SMART SCIENCE

Materials

Robert Snedden

First published in Great Britain by Heinemann Library, Halley Court, Jordan Hill, Oxford OX2 8EJ a division of Reed Educational and Professional Publishing Ltd.
Heinemann is a registered trademark of Reed Educational & Professional Publishing Ltd.

OXFORD MELBOURNE AUCKLAND
JOHANNESBURG BLANTYRE GABORONE
IBADAN PORTSMOUTH (NH) USA CHICAGO

Designed by Visual Image, Taunton
Illustrations by Paul Bale and Jane Watkins
Printed in Hong Kong

03 02 01 00
10 9 8 7 6 5 4 3 2 1

ISBN 0 431 03730 2
This title is also available in a hardback library edition (ISBN 0 431 03723 X).

British Library Cataloguing in Publication Data

Snedden, Robert
  Materials – (Smart science)
  1.Materials science – Juvenile literature
  I.Title
  500.2

Acknowledgements

The Publishers would like to thank the following for permission to reproduce photographs:
e.t. archive, p.16;
J. Allan Cash, pp.12, 15, 18, 20, 21, 23, 24, 25;
Raleigh, p.6;
Robert Harding Picture Library, (Mario Colonel) p.29;
Science Photo Library, (NASA) p.7; (Peter Menzel) p.11; (Astrid & Haans–Frieder Michler) pp.13, 19; (David Parker) p.14; (Rosenfeld Images Ltd) p.17; (Clive Freeman/Biosym Technologies) p.28;
The Stock Market, pp. 4, 5, 9, 22, 26, 27.

Cover photograph reproduced with permission of M2

Our thanks to Jim Drake for his comments in the preparation of this book.

Every effort has been made to contact copyright holders of any material reproduced in this book. Any omissions will be rectified in subsequent printings if notice is given to the Publisher.

CONTENTS

Any words appearing in the text in bold, like this, are explained in the glossary.

A MATERIAL WORLD

Every day we make use of a huge variety of materials. We all need to eat and drink, to have a place to live and clothes to wear. We use objects as we work and as we play and materials are used to make them all. We have taken rocks from the ground to build our homes, cut down trees to make furniture, taken **fibres** from plants and animals to make our clothes and created entirely new materials from **chemicals** to make all sorts of things such as pens, telephones and computers.

Many materials are used in a supermarket – including plastic and paper packaging, and glass and metal display cabinets.

The first materials

Humans have always made full and inventive use of the natural materials they can find around them. The first material to be used was probably stone. Early humans discovered that flint could be chipped to give a sharp edge that could be used for cutting. Flint tools have been discovered that are more than 200,000 years old. Today, there are a vast number of materials available because so many can be made artificially.

Manufacturing a car uses a lot of different materials – even wood.

It's a fact – Diamonds are forever!

The hardest wearing natural material of all is diamond. A diamond can only be cut and polished by other diamonds.

Manufacturing

Most materials have to be altered in some way before they can be used. Metals, fabrics and plastics are all **manufactured** from **raw materials**. Metals have to be extracted from rock **ores**, fabrics are woven, cut and stitched, plastics are made from chemicals obtained from **petroleum**. One of the earliest manufactured materials was **terracotta**. About 7000 years ago people discovered that soft clay could be altered into a harder-wearing, more useful material by baking it.

Scientists are always trying to improve materials and invent new ones to meet the changing demands of science and society.

Try this – Material quest

You need: a notebook and pencil, your home
What to do: Take a careful look around your home and try to list as many different types of material as you can. You may be surprised by how many you find. Can you see any metals or plastics?

THE RIGHT STUFF

When we use materials it is important that we choose the right material for the job. You would not want to ride on a bicycle made of rubber or wear a hat made of concrete!

On your bike!

In deciding what materials to use for a particular job, we have to consider the **properties** of the material and what we want it to do. A bicycle has to be strong enough to support the weight of the cyclist, light enough to be easy to push along, and it has to give a smooth ride. Metal tubes, made from steel, give the strength and lightness required for the frame and air-filled rubber tyres ensure that the cyclist has a comfortable ride over bumpy ground. The handlebars and saddle may be made from plastics, and oil is used to keep the moving parts running smoothly.

A bicycle needs to be made of strong, yet lightweight, materials.

Got a head? Get a hat!

The material used to make a hat will depend on the purpose of the hat. A woollen hat will keep your head warm in winter, a straw hat will shade you from the Sun in summer, and a strong plastic helmet will protect your head when you are riding your bike.

Space age materials

The requirements of space exploration have resulted in many new materials being developed. Space is a harsh place and tough materials are needed. Satellites are made using **honeycomb** structures of plastic and metal that combine strength with lightness. A metal honeycomb is sandwiched between thin sheets of plastic, strengthened with carbon **fibre** to form the body of the satellite. Lightness is important because the heavier the satellite, the more powerful the rocket has to be to get it into orbit.

A space shuttle orbiter returns to Earth. Ceramic tiles protected its titanium alloy body from the heat of re-entry into the **atmosphere**.

It's a fact – Metal hips

Titanium metal is often used to make artificial hip joints. It is ideal for this purpose because it is strong and also **unreactive**. This means that it will not wear away because it will not react with the **chemicals** in the patient's body.

Try this – Too hot to handle!

You need: a wooden spoon, a metal spoon, a plastic spoon and some hot water

What to do: Put all the spoons in the hot water with the handles sticking out. Which handle gets hottest? Which spoon would be the best for cooking with?

WHAT IS MATTER?

Everything that you can see and all the materials you make use of are made of **matter**. The air that you breathe, the water you drink, the food you eat, the book you hold in your hand, the bike you ride, and even you yourself, are all made of matter.

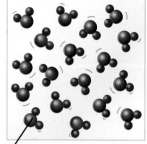

ice

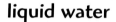

water molecule

Atoms

Anything that takes up space and has weight is matter. Matter is made of tiny particles called **atoms**. Ninety-four different kinds of atom exist in nature, and several others have been created in laboratories. Matter that is made up of just one kind of atom is a called an **element**.

liquid water

Atoms can group together in many different ways to make larger particles called **molecules**. A molecule can be a combination of two or more atoms of the same element or of atoms of different elements. Molecules made up of different atoms are called **compounds**.

steam

States of matter

Matter can exist in three forms or states – solid, liquid and gas. The molecules in a solid are packed closely together. A solid, such as a rock, has a definite **volume** and a definite shape that will not change.

In a solid the molecules are bound together. In a liquid they can move around and in a gas they are not attached to each other at all.

The molecules of a liquid are farther apart than those of a solid. A liquid, such as water, has a definite volume but it has no definite shape. If you pour water into a glass the water takes on the shape of the glass. The molecules of a gas are not bound to each other at all. A gas, such as oxygen, has no fixed shape or volume. It will quickly spread out into any container it is put into.

At these hot springs in Japan, water can be seen in its three states – snow, liquid water and steam.

We usually think of water as being a liquid, but when it freezes and becomes ice, it is a solid. When heated, water **evaporates** and turns into water vapour which is a gas. Ice, liquid water and water vapour are all made up of water molecules. They can exist in different states because of the way the molecules are spaced in each state. Most liquids can be cooled to form solids, most solids can be melted to form liquids, and most liquids can be heated to form gases.

It's a fact – Unnatural elements

17 elements have been created in laboratories. They are very unstable, so some only last for fractions of a second, and they do not exist in nature. They have no practical uses.

Try this – Different states
You need: some ice cubes, some hot water
What to do: Pour the hot water (liquid) on to the ice cubes (solid). You will see steam forming. Water gas, called water vapour, is invisible, but as it begins to cool back into a liquid it forms steam.

How Matter Behaves

All **matter** has distinct **properties**, such as its colour, density, or elasticity. The way that matter behaves – its appearance and the way it reacts with other materials – depends on how its **atoms** are arranged as well as on which atoms are in it.

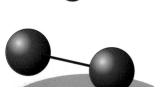

Two atoms of hydrogen link to form a single molecule of hydrogen.

Chemicals

All of the huge variety of **molecules** that make up us and the world around us are **chemicals**. The chemical properties of matter tell you how it will behave when you do different things to it. They also tell you what new combinations it can form when it reacts with other **elements** and **compounds**. Knowing the chemistry of a material will give you a good idea of what it will do under any conditions. For example, water is made up of hydrogen and oxygen. So, if hydrogen gas is burned with oxygen gas, water will always be made.

Two oxygen atoms link to form an oxygen molecule.

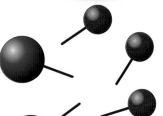

Compounds

Most of the chemicals we come across in everyday life are compounds. Compounds are made when two or more elements join together in a chemical reaction. Chalk, for example, is a compound of calcium, carbon and oxygen.

When oxygen and hydrogen react together, the bonds between the atoms are broken.

New bonds are formed as the hydrogen and oxygen atoms recombine to form molecules of water – which is a compound.

Compounds cannot be separated by physical means into the elements that make them up. You cannot separate salt into chlorine and sodium by heating, it would take another chemical reaction to separate them again.

Chemical reactions

Chemical reactions involve molecules coming apart and then coming together again in new ways to form compounds. Newly formed chemical compounds may have properties that are quite different from those of the original chemicals. The common salt we use in food is actually formed from sodium, which is a metal, and chlorine, which is a poisonous green gas!

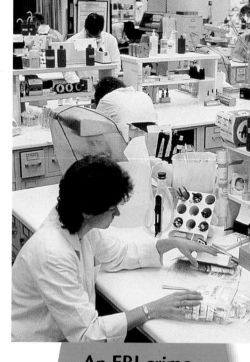

An FBI crime laboratory is equipped to analyse all sorts of chemicals.

It's a fact – Carbon compounds

Chemists have discovered more compounds that contain carbon than the total number of all the other kinds of compounds put together. Carbon can be found in a huge variety of things from plants and animals to vinegar, perfumes, alcohol and plastics.

Try this – It's a gas!

You need: a balloon, a small plastic drinks bottle, some vinegar, some bicarbonate of soda and a spoon

What to do: Fill the bottle about a quarter of the way up with vinegar. Using the spoon, put some bicarbonate of soda into the balloon. Hold the balloon carefully so it does not spill out. Stretch the neck of the balloon over the neck of the bottle, keeping the body of the balloon down as you do so to stop any bicarbonate from spilling out. Now quickly lift up the balloon so the bicarbonate spills into the vinegar. Carbon dioxide gas is released as the vinegar and bicarbonate react together. You can see this happening as your balloon starts to inflate!

CHANGING REACTIONS

Chemical reactions do not always go at the same speed or in the same direction. They can be made to go faster, or slower or be reversed.

Reaction rates

Some chemical reactions happen very quickly. A mixture of hydrogen gas and oxygen gas needs only a single spark to set off a fast, explosive reaction in which they combine to form water. Other reactions happen much more slowly. Iron slowly combines with oxygen in the air to form red iron oxide, called rust.

When a car rusts it is because oxygen in the air is slowly combining with the iron to form red iron oxide, or rust.

Reversible reactions

Some chemical reactions are known as reversible reactions – the change that has taken place can be undone or reversed. You can test this for yourself with a cabbage indicator. Ask an adult to help you with this experiment. Add some chopped red cabbage to some boiled distilled water and leave it to cool. Then strain the indicator liquid through a sieve into a jar. Add a little bicarbonate of soda to the liquid. Does it turn blue-green? Add some vinegar and the liquid will turn purple again. Add more vinegar and the liquid will turn red. Add more bicarbonate and the liquid will go purple. Chemical reactions are taking place between the bicarbonate of soda and the vinegar.

It's a fact – Living chemistry

Even while you are asleep, your body is busy breaking down the chemicals in your food and rearranging them to provide you with the energy you need to live and grow.

Non-reversible reactions

Most chemical reactions are non-reversible. Once the reaction has taken place it cannot be undone. If you set light to a piece of wood all you are left with is ash. There is no way that you can get the wood back again. The chemicals in the wood combine with oxygen when they burn, forming new **compounds**.

Nothing disappears when a chemical reaction takes place. If you could weigh all the soot and gases as well as the ash you would find that the total weight of the materials was the same as the weight of the piece of wood plus the oxygen it has combined with.

Burning, or combustion, is what happens when something combines rapidly with oxygen.

Try this – Rusting nails

You need: two iron nails, two airtight jars, tap water, cooled boiled water and vegetable oil

What to do: Put one nail in one jar with tap water. Seal the lid. Put the other nail in the other jar and slowly pour the boiled water over the nail. Then add a layer of vegetable oil on top. Leave for a few days. The nail in the tap water goes rusty, while the other does not. This is because tap water contains air. The boiled water does not contain air and the layer of oil stops any air entering. Water alone cannot make iron rust – oxygen must be present too.

MIXING AND SEPARATING

A mixture is something that contains two or more different materials that are mixed together, but which do not react chemically with each other to form new substances. A **compound** is made up of two or more different **elements** that have joined together to make a new substance.

In a **desalination** plant salt is removed from seawater to provide safe drinking water.

Mixtures

Many things can be added to each other to make mixtures. A fizzy drink is a mixture of liquid water, sugars and carbon dioxide gas, with some flavourings and colourings. **Petroleum** is a mixture containing many different oils. Mixtures can be separated by physical means. Salt can be separated from water by heating. The water **evaporates** and the salt is left behind. Rocks can be removed from garden soil by shaking the soil through a sieve that has holes big enough for the soil to pass through, but not the rocks. If oil and water are mixed together they will separate out because the oil is less dense than the water and will float on top of it.

It's a fact – Gold rush

People in search of riches would use huge pans to search for gold in rivers. A mixture of water, sand and gravel was swirled in the pan. Any heavy gold particles would sink to the bottom of the pan to be separated out from the mixture.

Solutions

Some solids will **dissolve** in water to give **solutions**. When you dissolve salt or sugar in water you are making a solution. The thing that does the dissolving, in this case the water, is called a **solvent** and the salt or sugar are **solutes**, the things that are dissolved. The solute separates out into different parts in the solution, but these parts will come together again unchanged if the solution evaporates. Some solids, such as sand and chalk, do not dissolve in water. They can be easily separated from water by filtering or sieving.

Try this – Salt extraction

You need: some salt, some warm water, a plastic beaker, a spoon and a saucer

What to do: Pour the water into the beaker and add a spoonful or so of salt. Stir until the salt has dissolved. Pour some of your solution into the saucer and leave it in a warm place. Eventually the water will evaporate and crystals of salt will be left behind. This shows that the salt and water did not react with each other but were simply mixed together.

METALS

Metals are all around you. Copper wire carries electricity through your home. Drinks cans are made of aluminium. Cars are made with steel, chromium, nickel and other metals. Iron and steel give strength to buildings and bridges. Life would be very different if we did not have metals.

Extremely thin sheets of gold, called gold leaf, have been used to decorate the pages of this book.

Metals and non-metals

Most of the **elements** are metals. With one exception, mercury, all metals are solids with high **melting points** and **boiling points**. Metals expand when they get hot and contract (get smaller) when they cool. You can see this happening in a thermometer as the mercury rises and falls in the tube as the temperature changes. Metals can be beaten into thin sheets or stretched out to form wires thinner than a human hair. Metals can be melted and poured into moulds to make a variety of objects. They are also good **conductors** of heat and electricity. Most non-metals are gases or solids with low melting points and, apart from carbon, they are poor conductors of electricity.

Most metals are shiny, when polished. Some metals will remain shiny for a very long time but others soon become dull or **tarnished**. This happens because the metal combines chemically with oxygen in the air.

Riches from rocks

Most metals combine with other elements to form **compounds** called **ores**. These are found in rocks. The metal has to be separated from the ore before it can be used, sometimes by crushing the ore and heating it to very high temperatures. This process is called smelting. Iron is obtained in this way. Other metals are extracted using electricity and **chemicals** to remove unwanted substances from the metal.

Many metals are extracted from ores heated to high temperatures in furnaces like this.

Alloys

Many metals can be made more useful by melting them and mixing them together to form **alloys**. Bronze is a very useful alloy made by combining tin and copper. It is harder than pure tin and more resistant to **corrosion**. Steel is made by combining iron with carbon (which is a non-metal) and some other metals. Stainless steel is made by adding chromium and nickel to iron. It does not rust and is often used for making cutlery.

It's a fact – More precious than gold?

Aluminium was once so difficult to extract that it was more precious than gold. Now a billion tonnes of bauxite, the aluminium ore, are extracted every year!

Try this – Metal fatigue

You need: an old metal spoon

What to do: Bend the spoon backwards and forwards many times. Eventually the metal will become so weak that the spoon will break in two. Metal fatigue is the weakening of metal caused by the repeated stresses and strains it receives in normal use.

BLACK GOLD

One of the most valuable and important materials in the world is **petroleum**. It is so valuable it has been called 'black gold'. Petroleum is also called crude oil or mineral oil. It is a **fossil fuel**, formed over millions of years from the remains of plants and animals.

Uses for petroleum

Petroleum has a huge number of uses. Fuels that come from petroleum provide the power for all forms of transport, including cars, trains, ships and aircraft. Fuel oil is also burned for heat. Many other useful products are made from petroleum, including cosmetics, explosives, paints and plastics.

Oil refinery

Petroleum is made up of a mixture of different oils and other materials. These are separated out at an oil refinery. First the petroleum is heated in closed containers. As the temperature is gradually increased each substance in the petroleum reaches its own **boiling point**.

In an oil refinery, like this one in Scotland, petroleum is split into a variety of products.

The gases produced by the boiling of each substance are drawn off from the container. They are then allowed to cool in separate containers to form liquids again. These liquids are the different petroleum products, such as gasoline (petrol), kerosene and heating oil.

Fantastic plastics

It would be nearly impossible to get through the day without using plastic in some shape or form. Most are made using ethene, which is a **compound** extracted from petroleum. Plastics can be stiff or bendy, hard or soft and they can be made into any shape or colour.

Just a few of the many everyday objects that are made from plastics.

It's a fact – Drake's Folly

The first oil well was drilled by Edwin L. Drake near Titusville, Pennsylvania, in 1859. The well was called 'Drake's Folly' because no one believed it would produce anything. But Drake proved his critics wrong and was soon getting 25 barrels of oil a day from his 21-metre deep well.

Try this – Make a badge!

Ask an adult to help you with this experiment.

You need: 330 ml of milk, vinegar, a saucepan, a tablespoon, a stove, a jar, a safety pin and a sieve

What to do: Warm the milk in the saucepan on the stove. Do not let it boil. Add a tablespoon of vinegar. A white rubbery material, called casein, forms in the milk. Put the sieve over the jar and pour the milk through it. The rubbery casein will be left behind. Leave it to set over a day or two. Push a safety pin into the plastic before it sets hard then paint it to make yourself a badge.

CERAMICS

Ceramics are plates, cups and other objects made from baked clay. The earliest known ceramics were made in the Middle East around 10,000 years ago. The process is simple. Clay is mixed with water to make it soft so that it can be shaped into an object. It is then 'fired' by putting it in a very high heat. Firing makes the clay hard.

Earthenware and stoneware

Earthenware is usually fired in a special oven, called a kiln, that can produce the very high temperatures needed. Fired clay is full of holes, called pores, which could make the ceramics leak. So earthenware is usually covered with a thin layer of glass, called a glaze, to stop it leaking. Stoneware is made with a mixture of clay and crushed rock. It is fired under heat strong enough to melt the crushed rock. The melted rock fills the pores in the clay so the stoneware does not have to be glazed.

An example of early Chinese porcelain dating from 1662.

Porcelain is made from white clay mixed with powdered rock. It is fired at very high temperatures and is extremely hard. It was invented in China over 1000 years ago. When porcelain first arrived in Europe from China in the 1400s, it was called China ware and the term 'china' is still used for porcelain objects.

It's a fact – Wedgwood blue

The first person to mass produce pottery was Josiah Wedgwood (1730–1795). Wedgwood's blue stoneware with raised white designs is still made today. It is so famous that we now use the term 'Wedgwood blue' to describe the particular shade of blue used for the pottery.

The potter's wheel

Most pottery today is mass-produced in factories where it can be shaped, fired and decorated on an assembly line. Mass-produced decorations are applied using paper transfers that are fixed to the piece when it is fired. However, there are still craftspeople who make pots by hand on the potter's wheel. Making pottery on a wheel is called throwing a pot. Pottery made on a wheel is always curved or round. Potters shape the clay with their fingers as the wheel spins.

A potter throws a pot using techniques that have been used for over 5000 years.

Try this – Make a pot

You need: modelling clay, a wooden board, a round-ended knife and a rolling pin

What to do: Roll out a piece of the clay and cut out a circle to form the base of your pot. Roll the remainder of the clay into long 'sausages' and build them up around the base to form a pot shape. Use the knife to smooth over the inside and outside of your pot. Leave it to harden and dry.

GLASS

Glass is a unique material. It can be transparent, **translucent** or **opaque**; it can be colourless or it can be coloured. It can be made into paper-thin sheets or drawn out into **fibres** finer than a human hair. It can be made into objects of art or into telescope mirrors weighing many tonnes.

A Japanese glass blower demonstrates skills that have been known for nearly 2000 years.

Glass-making

Most glass is made from sand (silica), soda (sodium oxide), and lime (calcium oxide) with other **compounds** sometimes being added to give the glass colour or to make it particularly clear. Often fragments of broken glass, called cullet, are added to the mixture. This is what happens to the bottles you recycle. The ingredients are well mixed, then blended together at a high temperature (1200 to 1600°C).

Glass must be shaped while it is still molten (semi-liquid) and very hot. This means that there is only a short time during which the glass can be worked. While it is molten, glass can be poured into moulds, rolled into sheets, or drawn into long threads or fibres by machine. The art of glass-blowing by hand has been around for nearly 2000 years. Melted glass is collected on the end of a hollow iron pipe about a metre or so long with a mouthpiece at one end. With this simple tool a skilled worker can create a variety of hollow glass objects.

A huge lens to focus the beam of a lighthouse – just one of the many uses of glass.

Sheet glass and plate glass

Sheet glass is the cheapest kind of glass used for making windows. It is made by drawing a wide ribbon of molten glass between large water-cooled rollers. Another method is to float molten glass in a layer on top of a bath of molten metal. For better quality glass, called plate glass, the sides of the sheets can be ground and polished by machine to get rid of any flaws.

It's a fact – Liquid windows

Glass is actually a very thick liquid! If you look closely at very old glass in an old building such as a church, you may be able to see that the glass is thicker at the bottom of the window than it is at the top. This is because the glass slowly flows down over hundreds of years.

Try this – The greenhouse effect

You need: a thermometer, a greenhouse or a car

What to do: One of the **properties** of glass is that it will let light pass through but traps heat very effectively. Take the temperature inside and outside a greenhouse, or on the windshield and the dashboard of a car (ask permission first!) on a sunny day. Is there a difference? Some gases in the **atmosphere**, such as carbon dioxide, trap heat in the same way that glass does. This is why the warming of the Earth's atmosphere is often called the **greenhouse effect**.

FABRICS

Many of the clothes we wear are made from a variety of fabrics. Fabrics are woven from many tiny strands called **fibres**. Natural fibres, from plants and animals, include cotton, wool, silk and linen. Many artificial or synthetic fibres are also used, including rayon, nylon and fibres made from glass. Glass fibres are often woven into fabrics to be used for upholstery because it makes them more fire-resistant.

An Australian shearer skilfully removes the fleece from a sheep.

Weaving

Natural fibres must be made into thread before they can be woven into fabrics. A textile is any fabric woven from threads or yarn. Linen textiles were first woven from the fibres of the flax plant thousands of years ago in Egypt. Woollen fabrics have been made from the fleece of sheep for over 5000 years. Textiles are often made from a combination of natural and artificial fibres, such as wool and polyester.

The weave is the pattern made by lacing the threads together into a fabric. There are three basic weaves – plain, twill and satin. Plain weave produces a sturdy cloth, such as muslin and tweed. The threads are woven evenly over and under in both directions. Twill weaves are hard-wearing. They are looser than plain weaves and are used in fabrics for

The skills of hand-weaving carpets are still practised in many countries.

heavier pieces of clothing such as coats and suits. Satin weaves have a smooth, flat surface. This gives satin an attractive sheen, but it is the weakest of the weaves.

Knitting and felting

Textiles can also be made by knitting and felting. In knitted fabric the yarn is twined together in a series of connected loops, giving a loose weave. Felting involves pressing the fabrics, usually wool, together under heat and pressure. Felts are heavy fabrics used for purposes such as insulating roof spaces in houses. Some fabrics are treated with **chemicals** to protect them from shrinking or staining, or to keep them from creasing or fading or the colours from running.

It's a fact – Clothes made from oil!

Nylon, the first synthetic fibre, was made by W.H. Carrothers in the USA in 1937. Nylon, which is used to make tights, waterproof jackets and other clothes, is made from **petroleum**, natural gas, air and water.

Try this – Waterproof fabrics

You need: samples of a variety of fabrics, such as cotton, wool, nylon and felt, a jug, water, a sieve and a container

What to do: Place the sieve over your container and line it with one of the fabrics. Pour water through the fabric. Try it with different fabrics. Which lets the water through easiest? Would you want to wear something made from this in the rain.

WOOD AND PAPER

It is hard to imagine a house that does not have wood in it somewhere. Furniture, doors, floorboards and often window frames are made from wood. In many parts of the world whole houses are made of wood.

Naturally versatile wood

Wood is one of the most useful and versatile of natural materials. It is light and strong and hard-wearing, making it an excellent building material. Wood generally has to be protected in some way, by applying paint or varnish, or protective **chemicals**. Insects such as woodworm and termites can cause damage, as can too much moisture.

The timber industry is an important part of the economy of countries such as Canada.

Woods are usually divided into either softwoods or hardwoods. Softwoods come from **coniferous** or evergreen trees, such as pines and firs. These are fast-growing trees that grow straight and tall, making them ideal for logging. Softwoods are used in building work and for making paper. Most softwoods are lighter than hardwoods.

Hardwoods, such as maple and walnut, come from broad-leaved, **deciduous** trees. Hardwoods are often very attractive woods and are used to make furniture among other uses.

Wood is pulped and rolled to make paper for a variety of uses in this papermill.

Paper-making

Paper is used for many purposes. We have paper bags, paper money, paper to write on, paper magazines and books.

The first paper, as we know it, was produced in China around AD 105. The Chinese mashed tree bark into a wet pulp and pressed it into flat sheets, which dried into paper. Today, paper is made in huge factories called paper mills, but the process is still largely the same. The cheapest paper is made entirely from wood pulp. Adding some cloth **fibres** produces better quality paper. The best paper is made entirely from cloth fibres, usually of linen or cotton.

It's a fact – Wasp inspiration

Early Chinese papermakers were inspired by the wasp! The wasp chews tiny pieces of wood into a pulp, which is mixed with saliva in the wasp's mouth. The wet pulp is smoothed into a thin sheet by the wasp. It dries to become paper which the wasp uses to build nests.

Try this – Paper-making

You need: some waste paper, water, a tray, fine wire mesh and a rolling pin

What to do: Tear the waste paper into very small pieces and soak it with water to make a

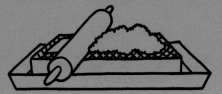

pulp. Spread the pulp over the wire mesh and roll it flat with the rolling pin over a tray (to catch the water). Leave to dry. Perhaps you could use your paper to make your own special greetings card.

FUTURE MATERIALS

We use materials today that would amaze people of 100 years ago. We have clothes made of waterproof Goretex, a **fibre** that keeps rain out but lets moisture from perspiration escape, cooking pots lined with non-stick Teflon; and sports rackets with strong but light carbon-fibre shafts.

Bucky balls and tubes

The search for new and better materials is always continuing. In 1985 a completely new form of carbon was discovered. It was called buckminsterfullerene, but this name is usually shortened to bucky balls, because the carbon forms ball-shaped **molecules**. Material scientists are still exploring ways in which this fascinating new material can be put to use. Richard Smalley, the discoverer of bucky balls, has found a way of creating bucky tubes, **conductive** wire that is 100,000 times thinner than a human hair. One day they could be used to make incredibly tiny electric circuits.

A computer graphic showing the structure of a buckminsterfullerene molecule.

Nanotechnology

Today, some of the most exciting scientific work on materials is being done on a very small scale indeed. The **properties** of a material depend on how the **atoms** that make up that material are arranged.

A diamond, the graphite in your pencil and a lump of coal are all carbon, but with the atoms arranged differently. Imagine if we could put atoms just where we want them. Obviously we can shift atoms around in huge numbers – you move billions and billions of atoms every time you pick something up – but the newly emerging field of **nanotechnology** could give us the ability to move a single molecule at a time.

One day it may be possible to construct microscopic machines, called nanobots, that could rearrange the molecules in ordinary household rubbish to make new items, such as food and clothes. Medical nanobots could be injected into the bloodstream to detect and destroy disease-causing germs and to repair damaged parts of the body.

New hard-wearing 'breathable' materials such as Goretex are popular with climbers and skiers.

It's a fact – Light aircraft

In the future nanotechnology may help us to build diamond-fibre aircraft that would weigh a fiftieth of present-day aircraft, but be just as strong. These superlight aircraft would use up a lot less fuel.

Try this – Recycling

You need: to be alert!

What to do: No matter how clever we get at making new materials we still need to conserve our supplies of **raw materials**. We can do this by recycling. Household paper, glass and tins can all be processed and used again. Find out where you nearest recycling centre is and encourage your friends and family to recycle as much household waste as they can.

Glossary

alloy mixture of two or more metals, or of a metal and a non-metal

atmosphere blanket of gases which surrounds the Earth

atom tiny particle from which all materials are made; the smallest part of an element that can exist

boiling point temperature at which a liquid changes into a gas

chemicals substances that can join together and mix with other substances; all of the elements and compounds that make up the materials around us

compound substance that contains atoms of two or more elements

conductive showing the ability to conduct electricity or heat

conductor substance that conducts electricity or heat

coniferous trees that are mostly evergreen and keep their leaves throughout the year

corrode/corrosion when the surface of a metal is attacked by a chemical, such as oxygen rusting iron, it is said to corrode

deciduous trees that shed their leaves at the end of the growing season

desalination remove salt from seawater to make it suitable for drinking

dissolve make something go into solution

element substance that cannot be broken down into simpler substances by chemical reactions; an element is made up of just one type of atom

evaporate change into a vapour or gas

fibre long, thread-like material that can be spun and woven to make textiles; some fibres are natural, from plants and animal fur, others are artificial, such as nylon

fossil fuel fuel that has been formed over millions of years from the remains of plants and animals that lived long ago; coal, petroleum and natural gas are fossil fuels

greenhouse effect warming of the Earth by heat trapped in the atmosphere by gases such as carbon dioxide and water vapour

honeycomb series of six-sided shapes made by honeybees

manufactured something that is made by people, rather than being natural

matter anything that takes up space and has weight; all of the substances around us; matter can be solid, liquid or gas

melting point temperature at which a solid turns into a liquid

molecule two or more atoms combined together; a molecule with atoms that are the same is an element, if it has different atoms it is a compound

nanotechnology science and technology of building very small devices from single atoms and molecules

opaque something that does not let light pass through

ore rock from which metals can be obtained

petroleum one of the fossil fuels

property quality of a material which makes it suitable for a particular job

raw material material in its natural state

solute substance that dissolves in a solvent to form a solution

solution mixture in which molecules from a solute are mixed, or dissolved, in the molecules of a solvent

solvent a substance (usually a liquid) in which a solute is dissolved to form a solution

tarnished describes the surface of a metal that has become discoloured or corroded

terracotta hard clay used in pottery and in buildings

translucent allows some light to pass through

unreactive describes something that will not easily react with other substances

volume amount of space that something takes up

INDEX